Rat Horoscope 2024

By
IChingHun FengShuisu

*Copyright © 2024 By IChingHun FengShuisu
All rights reserved*

Table of Contents

Introduce 5
Year of the Rat (Fire) | (1936) & (1996) 7
   Overview 7
   Career and Business 9
   Financial 10
   Family 11
   Love 12
   Health 13
Year of the Rat (Earth) | (1948) & (2008) 15
   Overview 15
   Career and Business 16
   Financial 17
   Family 18
   Love 19
   Health 19
Year of the Rat (Golden) | (1960) 20
   Overview 20
   Career and Business 21
   Financial 21
   Family 23
   Love 24
   Health 25
Year of the Rat (Water) | (1972) 26
   Overview 26
   Career and Business 27
   Financial 28
   Family 29

- Love 30
- Health 31

Year of the Rat (Wood) | (1984) 32
- Overview 32
- Career and Business 33
- Financial 34
- Family 35
- Love 36
- Health 37

Chinese Astrology Horoscope for Each Month 39
- Month 12 in the Tiger Year (6 Jan 24 - 3 Feb 24) 39
- Month 1 in the Dragon Year (4 Feb 24 - 5 Mar 24) 41
- Month 2 in the Dragon Year (6 Mar 24 - 5 Apr 24) 44
- Month 3 in the Dragon Year (6 Apr 24 - 5 May 24) 46
- Month 4 in the Dragon Year (6 May 24 - 5 Jun 24) 48
- Month 5 in the Dragon Year (6 Jun 24 - 6 Jul 24) 50
- Month 6 in the Dragon Year (7 Jul 24 - 7 Aug 24) 53
- Month 7 in the Dragon Year (8 Aug 24 - 7 Sep 24) 55
- Month 8 in the Dragon Year (8 Sep 24 - 7 Oct 24) 58
- Month 9 in the Dragon Year (8 Oct 24 - 6 Nov 24) 60
- Month 10 in the Dragon Year (7 Nov 24 - 6 Dec 24) 62
- Month 11 in the Dragon Year (7 Dec 24 - 5 Jan 24) 65

Amulet for The Year of the Rat 68

Introduce

The character of people born in the year of the rat

Rats prefer to live in packs. You have a large community as a result of your habitual politeness. There are numerous connections. On the other hand, allowing anyone to enter into a deep relationship with each other is extremely rare. You appear to be a patient individual who is unconcerned about the end of the world. But you're nervous because of the relaxed atmosphere. You value your solitude and privacy. Anyone who enters your life uninvitedly will be dizzy from your sharp lips. Rats are self-centered, stubborn creatures who prefer to solve problems on their own. Personal transactions where no one will threaten or cause problems. Parents who enjoy playing with their children are known as rat parents.

People born in this year are typically smart, intelligent, and capable of surviving. Beliefs of the ancient Chinese If there are mice in the house, it is believed that food will be plentiful throughout the year.

Strength:
Rat people have a high level of intelligence. It also conceals the habit of cheating and preferring to socialize first. People born in this year are frequently successful entrepreneurs.

Weaknesses:
As a result of being overly ambitious, frequently leads to mistakes.

Love:
People born this year have less romantic love as a result of a mischievous child's personality. People born in this year, on the other hand, simply love someone who adores and despise someone who worships. As a result, those who want to break the heart of someone born this year should reconsider their urgent plan. People born in this year are lovely. However, the love of the year is not always long-lasting. We have a simple love habit. The habit is not stubborn, prefers consistency, and is frequently obsessed with eroticism.

Suitable Career:
People born in the year of the rat are classified as belonging to the water element. Opening a store, selling liquor, beer, and seafood, opening a shipping company, building a boat, developing a tour company, a diplomat, an accountant, a finance company, a salesman, a broker, a negotiating job, a job related to the sale of metal and jewelry, selling jewelry or machinery, etc. are all appropriate occupations for those born in the year of the rat.

Year of the Rat (Fire) | (1936) & (1996)
"The Rat in the Barn" is a person born in the year of the Rat at the age of 88 years (1936) and 28 years (1996)

Overview
    For seniors of this age, Because the planets that will circle into your destiny home this year are "nine satellites" that will have a direct impact on health and accidents. As a result, the

most important problem you must address this year is health. Whether it is food that must be clean and sanitary. That includes getting adequate sleep. You should both strive to relax your minds. Don't be overly concerned about what's to come. You should also go to worship the Buddha on a regular basis. Make merit and create merit It will make your life happier, and many things will go more smoothly.

For those destined to be 28 years old in the Year of the Rat, this year is considered an auspicious year for you. You should work diligently and build yourself up to stability. Because the house of destiny appears to have auspicious stars orbiting to shine. Work is progressing. Business will prosper. Easy to buy, easy to sell, profitable Therefore, you should not let the good times of this year pass by without something in your hand. However, during the year you should be careful of the influence of malevolent stars that orbit and disturb your house of destiny as well. "Dao Kiam Hong" (star of sharp sword), Dao Tai Im (star of moon) and Dao Xiaoae (star of small danger). As a result, the most essential thing in your life cycle is to develop caution and alertness. Be wary of unforeseen threats. Because you are likely to suffer as a result of being encircled. Or the danger of being in a bad circumstance and unable to find a way out. This includes being cautious of mishaps while at work and when traveling.

Career and Business

There are no concerns about this year's work. Because you will be on the path to success. Those who work full-time will advance in their positions. Those who own a business will see more sales and revenue. Capable of expanding company, opening additional branches, increasing productivity, and adding new production. The 12th Chinese month (6 Jan. - 3 Feb.), the 3rd Chinese month (4 Apr. - 4 May), the 7th Chinese month (7 Aug. - 6 Sep.), and the 11th Chinese month (6 Dec. '24 - 4 Jan. '25) are all good months for your profession. However, you should be cautious during these months since work and investments will face challenges. These months include the 2nd Chinese month (5 March - 3 April), the 5th

Chinese month (5 June - 5 July), and the 6th Chinese month (6 July - 6 August). & China's eighth month (7 September - 7 October). When signing an employment contract or taking a job, you must be wary of little details that might be exploited and cause you to struggle later. Be wary of intruders who may try to con you out of your money. You should also refrain from beginning a new career. Investing in equities and other areas during the months mentioned earlier.

Financial

This year's financial fortunes are expected to be favorable. Income will be generated in a variety of ways. Both receiving the benefits of old concerns and investing in new things produce a growing total. As a result, you must be diligent in your task. The more you do, the more money you will receive. They are the 12th Chinese month (6 Jan. - 3 Feb.), the 3rd Chinese month (4 Apr. - 4 May), the 7th Chinese month (7 Aug. - 6 Sep.), and the 11th month of China (6 Dec. '24 - 4 Jan. '25). However, for the money expected from gambling, I would want to caution you with good intentions. If you are greedy, your riches will likely vanish.

Finances will be tight and there will be unexpected expenses during the months that you should be cautious, including the 2nd month of China (5 Mar. - 3 Apr.), the 5th month of China (5 Jun. - 5 Jul.), the 6th month of China (6 Jul. - 6 Aug.), and the 8th month of China (7 Sep. - 7 Oct.), where you are prohibited from signing any type of guarantee. Furthermore, be wary of fraudsters that promise you incentives in order to deceive you. If you fall into investing or are involved in an illegal operation, even if the reward is good, you will end up in prison, therefore you should not take the chance.

Family
This year's family horoscope has experienced a visit from favorable energy. Moving into a new house or habitation would be favorable for you. There will also be a chance to welcome new members to the home. There will also be auspicious work done in the dwelling. This year is a middle level for family and friends. Even if you occasionally receive assistance from pals.

But, in the end, "you are your own self," therefore when you receive appropriate counsel, it must be tailored to each individual's ability. However, because the home is influenced by negative constellations, there will be disturbed happenings throughout the year. As a result, you should be extra cautious in the next months: The 2nd Chinese month (5 Mar. - 3 Apr.), the 5th Chinese month (5 Jun. - 5 Jul.), the 6th Chinese month (6 Jul. - 6 Aug.), and the 8th Chinese month (7 Sep. - 7 Oct.) You should be cautious of any unforeseen mishaps that may occur to household members. Care for the elderly in the home, and be wary of possessions being destroyed, lost, or stolen.

Love

You will find both positive and unpleasant things in your love horoscope. Even if your husband and lover would take good care of you and support you in your profession. However, he cannot be self-centered unless he listens to the perspectives of others. Especially during the months when your love is relatively frail and conflicts are common, such as the 2nd Chinese month (5 Mar. - 3 Apr.), the 5th Chinese month (5 Jun. - 5 Sep.), the 6th Chinese month (6 Jul. - 6 Aug.), and the 8th Chinese month (7 Sep.- 7 Oct.). Keep an eye out for misconceptions. Each party comprehended it without any debate or revision. Do not intervene or serve as a third party in other people's relationships, and avoid going to places of amusement that bring illnesses back to cause difficulty.

Health

The chosen individual for this year is in poor physical health. Because your immune system is weak, you are vulnerable to seasonal infectious disorders such as allergies and other infectious diseases. As a result, the intended individual must exercise caution should this ailment become a problem. This prevents work from progressing indefinitely. During the month, you should pay greater attention to your physical health. Because it is easier to fall and become ill during the 2nd Chinese month (5 Mar. - 3 Apr.), the 5th Chinese month (5 Jun. - 5 Jul.), the 6th Chinese month (6 Jul. - 6 Aug.), and the 8th Chinese month (7 Sep. - 7 Oct.). While working with sharp equipment or tools.

To avoid damage and bleeding, you should exercise utmost caution. Don't be reckless when driving a car on the road. It will aid in the reduction of accidents and losses.

Year of the Rat (Earth) | (1948) & (2008)

"The Rat in the beam" is a person born in the year of the Rat at the age of 76 years (1948) and 16 years (2008)

Overview

This year is another fantastic one for the 16-year-old kid. They are still residing in educational institutions at this age. As a result, you should aim to learn both inside and outside of the classroom. Keep up with the times by learning more about new topics. Gather experiences for the future. Furthermore, this year, an auspicious star called "Buen Chiang" is orbiting the house of destiny to aid boost education. As a result, if the mind is not led astray by temptation, academic outcomes will be successful and development will be made. However, you should not be reckless. Thinking arrogantly, believing you are so good, failing to review, and lacking self-improvement in numerous areas. Finally, even a good star will assist you. However, you can also fall behind.

Career and Business

For teens, employment is education, therefore they must pay close attention because their surroundings are continually changing. If you become engrossed in a group of friends and become distracted by technology stimuli, your academic performance will lag behind that of your classmates. As a result, you should focus more on being a leader rather than a follower. During the month when both work and studies are down and destiny in both age cycles, including the 2nd Chinese month (5 Mar. - 3 Apr.), the 5th Chinese month (5 Jun. - 5 Jul.), the 6th Chinese month (6 Jul. - 6 Aug.), and the 8th month of China (7 Sep. - 7 Oct.), must be extremely cautious. Where the destiny of teens must be steadfast and not allow others sway them wrong. As for whether the senior person meets the requirements to sign any contract agreements. You should thoroughly review the contract's finer points. So that you will not be bound by future contracts. For the months when work and studies go smoothly, such as the 12th Chinese month (6 Jan. - 3 Feb.), the 3rd Chinese month (4 Apr.- 4 May.), the 7th Chinese month (7 Aug. - 6 Sep.), and the 11th Chinese month (6 Dec. 24 - 4 Jan. 25).

Financial
This year's financial fortunes are not stable, so here's what can help: Economical spending and careful spending planning, cutting down on unnecessary expenses and trying to find extra income from additional hobbies. Because otherwise, they would probably face a financial crisis. Especially during the months when financial liquidity will shrink, including 2nd Chinese month (5 Mar. - 3 Apr.), 5th Chinese month (5 Jun. - 5 Jul), 6th Chinese month (6 Jul. – 6 Aug.) and the 8th month of China (7 Sep. – 7 Oct.), so do not lend money to others or sign financial guarantees. Do not be greedy or covet things that do not belong to you. Including prohibiting all types of gambling. Do not invest in illegal and high-risk businesses. For the months in which finances return to flow smoothly, they are the 12th Chinese month (6 Jan. - 3 Feb.), the 3rd Chinese month (4 Apr. - 4 May), the 7th Chinese month (7 Aug. – 6 Sep.)

and the 11th Chinese month (6 Dec. 2024 – 4 Jan. 2025)

Family

This year's family is at ease with patronage power. You meet the requirements for purchasing pricey real estate for your home. There is also a lucky time to move into a new home or apartment. A fortunate event will take place both within and outside the house. You could get more people in the house. But because terrible stars will be surrounding you throughout the year. This will have an impact on your health as well as the health of the elderly in your household. Keep an eye out for any unforeseen incidents in the house. The 2nd Chinese month (5 Mar. - 3 Apr.), the 5th Chinese month (5 Jun. - 5 Jul.), the 6th Chinese month (6 Jul. - 6 Aug.), and the 8th Chinese month (7 Sep. - 7 Oct.) are the months when there will be instability inside the family. Furthermore, be aware that there will be disagreements with individuals around. Be wary of subordinates or servants who cause trouble.

Love

    This year of love for the adolescent destiny appears to be a lovely one. You'll discover an invitation to satisfy others. It may easily lead your imagination astray in a variety of situations, so you must be cautious and know how to quiet your mind properly. Don't be too quick. Otherwise, you must understand how to avoid it. Don't only take care of yourself and cause issues for your family. Especially during the months when issues are more prone to develop, such as the 2nd Chinese month (5 Mar. - 3 Apr.), the 5th Chinese month (5 Jun. - 5 Jul.), the 6th Chinese month (6 Jul. - 6 Aug.), and the 8th Chinese month (7 Sep. - 7 Oct.).

Health

    Especially during the months that fateful people in both age cycles must be especially careful and take care of themselves, namely the 2nd Chinese month (5 Mar. - 3 Apr.), the 5th Chinese month (5 Jun. - 5 Jul.), the 6th Chinese month (6 Jul. - 6 Aug.), and the 8th Chinese month (7 Sep. - 7 Oct.) to be more careful of injury from accidents both while traveling and driving car.

Year of the Rat (Golden) | (1960)

"The Rat on the Beam of the House" is a person born in the year of the Rat at the age of 64 years (1960)

Overview

This year is considered auspicious for persons born in the Year of the Rat who will be 64 years old. Your home will get auspicious fortune. This will encourage the inside of your home to be able to handle auspicious and pleasant occurrences. Whether it's a birthday party, a housewarming party, or a celebration of the accomplishments of children and grandkids. Both of you will have the qualifications for purchasing pricey real estate. There is a possibility to relocate to a new home. However, throughout the year, there came a collection of malevolent stars that orbited to destroy and disturb the house of fate, particularly "Dao Kiam Hong (Star of the Laem Sword) and the Nine Satellites. (Blue Dog Star)," all of which had a negative impact.

Career and Business

This year's employment and business for the chosen person is highly tumultuous, up and down. You must be cautious that there will be an intervention that will result in significant modifications to your job. As a result, if there is a lack of proper operational planning or if fraudsters are not avoided, You may make a mistake that causes you to have problems. This year, you must keep a carefree attitude, especially during the months when the career stars are falling, specifically the 2nd Chinese month (5 Mar. - 3 Apri.), the 5th Chinese month (5 Jun. - 5 Jul.), the 6th Chinese month (6 Jul. - 6 Aug.), and the 8th Chinese month (7 Sep. - 7 Oct.). You should do well during these months. Don't get in the way of other people's efforts. Don't be duped into trusting anybody without first analyzing the evidence. Be cautious while signing labor contract agreements. You can find yourself in a difficult situation.

Financial

This year, you must keep a carefree attitude, especially during the months when the career stars are falling, specifically the 2nd Chinese month (5 Mar.- 3 Apri.), the 5th Chinese month (5 Jun. - 5 Jul.), the 6th Chinese month (6 Jul. - 6 Aug.), and the 8th Chinese month (7 Sep. - 7 Oct.). You should do well during these months. Don't get in the way of other people's efforts. Don't be duped into trusting anybody without first analyzing the evidence. Be cautious while signing labor contract agreements. You can find yourself in a difficult situation. There will be unexpected costs, especially during the months when the financial stars are in decline and you must be cautious, such as the 2nd Chinese month (5 Mar. - 3 Apr.) and the 5th Chinese month (5 Jun. - 5 Jul.). The Chinese 6th month (6 Jul. - 6 Aug.) and Chinese 8th month (7 Sep. - 7 Oct.) should be cautious with their money. To avoid financial difficulties, avoid becoming greedy. Also, avoid investing in areas in which you lack knowledge and do not lend money to others. The months in which financial luck returns to flow easily are the 12th Chinese month (6 Jan. - 3 Feb.), the 3rd Chinese month (4 Apr. - 4 May), the 7th Chinese month (7 Aug. - 6 Sep.), and the 11th Chinese month (6 Dec. '24 - 4 Jan. '25).

Family

This year's family horoscope has experienced a visit from favorable energy. You will be able to purchase costly assets. There is an ideal time to move into a new house, or the house may welcome new members, or an auspicious celebration for children and grandkids may be held. However, you should exercise caution during the months of chaos and unrest in the home, such as the 2nd Chinese month (5 Mar. - 3 Apr.), the 5th Chinese month (5 Jun. - 5 Jul.), the 6th Chinese month (6 Jul. - 6 Aug.), and the 8th Chinese month (7 Sep. - 7 Oct.), because two evil stars with Im power, namely the Tai Im star and the Nine Celestial star, appear. Harassing the home of destiny, resulting in the first thing to be cautious of is the health issues of the individuals in the house. The second consideration is home security. Be wary about valuables in your home being lost or stolen. As a result, you should examine the home's equipment on a frequent basis. If it is damaged, it should be fixed or replaced. This includes tightening security measures for members of the house.

Love

Conflicts and disputes are common in love horoscopes throughout the first half of the year. After the middle of the year, you will be granted auspicious authority and patronage. As a result, love begins to flow freely and without interruption. You should both regard it as a nice moment, a chance to take your husband and lover on a sightseeing tour to a distant nation or to travel to achieve merit together. It is a method of making love sweeter in old age. However, you should exercise caution during the months when love is delicate and might cause issues, such as the 2nd Chinese month (5 Mar. - 3 Apr.), the 5th Chinese month (5 Jun. - 5 Jul.), 6th Chinese month (6 Jul. - 6 Aug.) and 8th Chinese month (7 Sep. - 7 Oct.). You should be firm throughout this time. Avoid visiting to entertainment establishments and do not listen to gossip. It will make love suspect and lead to unneeded disputes. You should not meddle in the family lives of others.

Health

This year's senior destinies must not overlook the importance of health. This is due to a difficulty with an underlying disease or the emergence of an underlying disease. You should also be cautious about not getting enough rest. Perhaps by working hard or visiting too many receptions, leading the body to grow exhausted, sickness will appear and demand it. You should be especially cautious about high blood pressure, stomach sickness, intestinal disease, and blood clots. If something unexpected is discovered, it is a warning indication. See a doctor as soon as possible. Don't wait too long for some diseases to have a greater impact than before. The months to be more cautious about accidents are the 2nd Chinese month (5 Mar. - 3 Apr.), the 5th Chinese month (5 Jun. - 5 Jul.), the 6th Chinese month (6 Jul. - 6 Aug.), and the 8th Chinese month (7 Sep. - 7 Oct.).

Year of the Rat (Water) | (1972)

"The Rat in the field" is a person born in the year of the Rat at the age of 52 years (1972)

Overview

This age cycle is another fortunate year for people born in the Year of the Rat. You will be bestowed with prosperity, power, renown, and prestige. It's because a once-in-a-lifetime chance came calling. Both sponsors are encouraging. As a result, you should not allow good moments pass you by without something returning. Throughout the year, you will meet friends who will provide you advise and work contacts, you will start a new business or employment, or you will be able to invest in new enterprises. Profits will increase brilliantly until you can construct a cohesive business and take it to the next level. However, you must use extreme caution. Because there are unfortunate stars in the house of destiny that have bad repercussions. "Dao Kiam Hong" (Laem Krabi Star) has a strong impact that may rapidly spread, causing mishaps while working or traveling. It will also provide the owner of the fate the opportunity to be irresponsible and forget himself for a little while, as well as to be briefly disloyal. You should have greater faith in yourself against any vices and take better care of your marriage. Despite the fact that running business necessitates going out and meeting people. There will be a launch celebration. Including a variety of certifications Some objects may require attention. You must exercise caution in this program since "Dao Marot Huai" is waiting for the appropriate opportunity to strike you this year. As a result, whether attending social events or traveling to entertainment places, extreme caution is advised. Be cautious of becoming infected with an illness that will cause problems and influence many other things.

Career and Business

This year's effort will bring riches, fortune, renown, prestige, and position. You will also get encouragement and assistance from both the top and bottom levels until you are able to successfully run your firm in accordance with your objectives. If you can locate an heir or a trustworthy individual to assist you this time. It will make your work appear to have wings, allowing you to achieve success sooner and extend your work more broadly. The months that support and promote your work to be prosperous are the 12th Chinese month (6 Jan. - 3 Feb.), the 3rd Chinese month (4 Apr. - 4 May), the 7th Chinese month. (7 Aug. - 6 Sep.) and the 11th Chinese month (6 Dec. '24 - 4 Jan. '25), but be careful during the following months where the career stars turn downward, namely the 2nd Chinese month (5 Mar. – 3 Apr.), 5th Chinese month (5 Jun. – 5 Jul.), 6th Chinese month (6 Jul. – 6 Aug.), and 8th Chinese month (7 Sep. - 7 Oct.) that you should delay investing because you are likely to be deceived.

Financial

This year will be prosperous financially. Make your face pleasant, revenue inflow will come in two forms: direct sales income or money from extra employment, including windfalls. This year's lucky and prosperous months are the 12th Chinese month (6 Jan. - 3 Feb.), the 3rd Chinese month (4 Apr. - 4 May), the 7th Chinese month (7 Aug. - 6 Sep.), and the 11th Chinese month (6 Dec. '24 - 4 Jan. '25). However, there will be an intervention event throughout the year that will cause a certain amount of capital to flow out. Be wary of con artists. As a result, if you do not have money set up for emergencies. It is impossible to be in a condition of crisis. Especially during the 2nd Chinese month (5 Mar. - 3 Apr.), the 5th Chinese month (5 Jun. - 5 Jul.), the 6th Chinese month (6 Jul. - 6 Aug.), and the 8th Chinese month (7 Sep. - 7 Oct.).

Family

There will be favorable energy visiting the household this year. There is an auspicious moment to enter a new house, move into a new house, purchase expensive property, perform an auspicious event in the house, or welcome new members into the house. However, due to the evil star Guangji attacking the family money base throughout the year. Unexpected incidents and disagreements should be avoided. Especially during the months when the family will be more chaotic, such as the 2nd Chinese month (5 Mar. - 3 Apr.), the 5th Chinese month (5 Jun. - 5 Jul.), the 6th Chinese month (6 Jul. - 6 Aug.), and the 8th Chinese month (7 Sep. - 7 Oct.). You should be wary of anyone in the house getting into an argument with the neighbors. It forces the couple to gaze at each other's faces again. Keep an eye out for valuables that have been damaged, misplaced, or stolen.

Love

    This year's love is smooth and lovely. Those of you who are still unmarried will have another year full of charm. Because the opposite sex will want to know and become closer to you. The chosen individual who already has a significant other will have a second chance to take their loved one on a trip abroad or on a honeymoon. to deepen the love bond However, you should exercise caution during particular months of the year, such as the 2nd Chinese month (5 Mar. - 3 Apr.), the 5th Chinese month (5 Jun. - 5 Jul.), 6th Chinese month (Jul. 6 - Aug. 6) and 8th Chinese month (7 Sep. - 7 Oct.)

Health

This year's general health is fairly good. It's like having auspicious power to assist build the body. But you can't be careless about food hygiene, drinking alcohol, smoking excessively, or eating anything in excess. It frequently has a detrimental impact on health. This year, be wary of gastritis, intestinal sickness, food poisoning, and seasonal infectious disorders. The months when you should pay particular attention to your health are the 2nd Chinese month (5 Mar. - 3 Apr.), the 5th Chinese month (5 Jun. - 5 Jul.), and the 6th month. China (6 Jul. - 6 Aug.) and the 8th month of China (7 Sep. - 7 Oct.). When traveling or conducting business, keep an eye out for accidents.

Year of the Rat (Wood) | (1984)

"The rat in the mountains" is a person born in the year of the Rat at the age of 40 years (1984)

Overview

This life cycle is for the Year of the Rat horoscope because the primary planets that orbit into your horoscope this year are "Ninth satellite" (sky dog star), so even if the overall image will be favorable, there will be a helpful direction. However, whether thinking, reading, or doing any activity, you cannot be impatient and act on your emotions. It will bring more harm than good. Before taking action, it is still necessary to assess and consider the larger picture in all areas. Recognize the time and opportunity that comes your way, and then walk away. This year's work and business will also be supported and promoted. You may also buy pricey property. There is an opportune moment to move into a new home. You must, however, exercise prudence. Because there are unfortunate stars in the house of destiny that have bad consequences, such as the Tai Im star and the Heng Sua star, which tend to have a negative influence in many issues. The most important thing to keep in mind is the risk of an accident. Interference at work caused by unexpected events or the risk of being bullied or attacked by a minor or someone close to you. Furthermore, you are forbidden from investing in enterprises that are disrespectful or unlawful. This includes being wary of being duped into participating in criminal conduct without your awareness. So, regardless of who motivates you to do anything. Let's start with its roots. In order to avoid disaster and crossfire.

Career and Business

Work that includes trade This year is deemed fortunate for you to shine and demonstrate your abilities. Both discovered the route to riches; thus, you should not sit idle without following it carefully. Because such a lovely chance does not come along very frequently. Increasing investment, both internally and outside, will offer you profit and revenue. The benefits will be large on both counts. Especially during the 12th Chinese month (6 Jan. - 3 Feb.), the 3rd Chinese month (4 Apr. - 4 May), the 7th Chinese month (7 Aug. - 6 Sep.), and the 11th Chinese month (6 Dec. '24 - 4 Jan. '25). The months to avoid investing in include the 2nd Chinese month (5 Mar. - 3 Apr.), the 5th Chinese month (5 Jun. - 5 Jul.), the 6th Chinese month (6 Jul. - 6 Aug.), and the 8th Chinese month (7 Sep. - 7 Oct.). When creating various contract papers, you should ensure that they are clear and thorough. Because you could be taken advantage of and end yourself in a fight later.

Financial

The destined person's financial fortune is nicely spread out this year, and cash inflows will come in from a variety of sources. Salary and sales revenue with extra money or fortune from gambling. Your money will run smoothly this month. It is also a good time to invest in expanding results in various areas, such as the 12th Chinese month (6 Jan. - 3 Feb.), the 3rd Chinese month (4 Apr. - 4 May), the 7th Chinese month (7 Aug. - 6 Sep.), and the 11th Chinese month (6 Dec. '24 - 4 Jan. '25), where you can choose to invest the money in the planned business. Expect to get a good return on your investment. However, there are still several months this year where unanticipated intervening expenditures may emerge and harm liquidity, such as the 2nd Chinese month (5 Mar. - 3 Apr.). the 5th Chinese month (5 Jun. - 5 Sep.), the 6th Chinese month (6 Jul - 6 Aug.) and the 8th Chinese month (7 Sep.- 7 Oct.) It is illegal to allow people to borrow money or sign financial promises. Gamble, take risks, avoid doing or becoming engaged in illicit operations, and be wary of fraudsters.

Family
The family will be visited by favorable energy this year. Throughout the year, prominent individuals will come to visit the house as a sign of respect for the folks who live there. Both will have the option to purchase pricey items. There is an opportune moment to move into a new home. There is a chance to welcome new members into the family at home. It is an enhancement to the already fortunate base. However, you should exercise caution during the months when the family may confront

challenges, such as the 2nd Chinese month (5 March - 3 April) and the 5th Chinese month (5 June - 5 July). The Chinese sixth month (July 6 - August 6) and the Chinese eighth month (September 7 - October 7). Keep an eye out for kids or subordinates in the house getting into mischief with neighbors. Good partnerships must be sporadic. Take cautious not to overestimate your talents or disrespect others to the point of causing yourself anguish. You should also be cautious of destroying your belongings as a result of being misplaced or falling into a scammer's trap.

Love
This year, the fate's love standards are in jeopardy. However, if you sincerely love and want to marry, show some guts and you will be successful. However, if you have a partner or lover, this year you must be cautious of the bad stars assaulting you and leading you to become thoughtless and unconscious. It has caused fissures in a once-smooth affection. So don't go into problems or bring yourself into difficulty. Especially during the months when love is

quite fragile and arguments will easily occur, such as the 2nd Chinese month (5 Mar. - 3 Apr.), the 5th Chinese month (5 Jun. - 5 Jul.) 6th Chinese month (6 Jul. - 6 Aug.) and 8th Chinese month (7 Sep. - 7 Oct.) Make your heart firm. Don't listen to rumors and gossip. Love to trust your loved ones more than people who sound evil and behave well to stay on a good path. Don't go to entertainment venues. Because it will cause a cause of division.

Health

In terms of your health this year, the first half looks promising. Immunity will deteriorate after the middle of the year. As a result, you might be allergic to anything. Even though it was never before. Both will quickly grow unwell and will induce sickness. Whether it's a cold, a headache, gastrointestinal ailment, or something else. When consuming food, you should take care and pay attention to hygiene. Drinking and eating items that are harmful to the body should be avoided. Especially during the months when you should pay special attention to your health, such as the 2nd

Chinese month (5 Mar. - 3 Apr.) and the 5th Chinese month (5 Jun. - 5 Jul.). The sixth Chinese month (6 Jul. - 6 Aug.) and the 8th Chinese month (7 Sep. - 7 Oct.)

Chinese Astrology Horoscope for Each Month

Month 12 in the Rabbit Year (6 Jan 24 - 3 Feb 24)
Enter this month for the Year of the Rat's lucky person. Because they are moving to meet the months that help each other. As a result, an auspicious force exists to assist and urge many of the accumulated unpleasant issues to have a direction to be addressed and suddenly become brighter. If, on the other hand, you have planned your job from the beginning of the year, Set success objectives. It's preferable than wasting time without understanding where you're going. The first Chinese New Year firecrackers were let off. The fortunate power of the people of the Year of the Rat is thought to have begun.

Work and preparation for commencing a new job this month. May you have the fortitude to let go of the old and create something new and better. Change channels or improve trading methods It may be claimed that the more you do, the more prosperous you will get. Including investment in new branches. can take action

You can wait until the end of the year to collect your entire payout.

The financial horoscope for this month is in a position to get bountiful money. The consistent infusion of financial inflows is gratifying. Please be vigilant and persistent. Always seek to improve yourself and learn more. Don't be still. Allow the opportunity to slip away.

There is harmony in the household. Discovered the fortunate power of patronage and promoted a tranquil and happy family. The loving side is smooth. You will discover someone you love who will not displease you if you are single. It's called pointing out a bird. A stick is a stick.

Your health will improve. However, you should exercise greater caution when it comes to drinking and eating habits. Choose to consume nutritious foods that are good for your health. To avoid infectious infections

Family and friends are helpful. This month, you have the opportunity to meet with a trusted friend who will advise you on the best course of action for your investment. If you dare to take a step forward. At the end of the year, there is a propensity to sit and comfortably count money.

Support Days: 1 Jan., 5 Jan., 9 Jan., 13 Jan., 17 Jan., 21 Jan., 25 Jan., 29 Jan.
Lucky Days: 2 Jan., 14 Jan., 26 Jan.
Misfortune Days: 7 Jan., 19 Jan., 31 Jan
Bad Days: 8 Jan, 10 Jan, 20 Jan, 22 Jan,

Month 1 in the Dragon Year (4 Feb 24 - 5 Mar 24)
This month will bring you a combination of good and bad luck. This is due to the zodiac house moving to meet a group of malicious stars circling the house of destiny. What you should be aware of is that you should be cautious regarding home security. Including a number of unanticipated mishaps. However, you will get good fortune from the lucky stars that circle and shine together throughout the monsoon season. This will aid in the

transformation of bad to good, from heavy to light.

This is a good starting pay. However, gambling with windfalls, including stock lottery speculation, is still fraught with danger. The greatest method to avoid losing is to avoid being greedy when playing. Also, avoid becoming greedy while investing for unrealistically appealing profits. Because the repercussions will be insignificant.

In terms of labor, there are still challenges and hurdles that have developed throughout this time period. Please keep your voice down. Maintain your responsibilities in the fortress. Giving directions should be done in a reasonable manner. Using just electricity You may not always receive what you desire, and you may unintentionally suffer negative repercussions as a result.

There will be upheaval inside the family. Be aware that there may be health issues for members of the household. Be wary of burglars entering into your house or taking your belongings. For single folks, the love part is easy. Those who have a family who is afraid of the bad stars, on the other hand, become passionate and loyal to one cause until the family is split apart.

Your horoscope is in good health. Just be wary of past ailments reappearing or silent diseases threatening to emerge. It doesn't matter if it's heart disease, liver illness, or food poisoning.

Do not intervene in other people's family connections, especially with relatives and friends. For starting a new career, investing in stocks, and making other types of investments. This month is not going well. It will be beneficial if you can take a break or avoid it.

Support Days: 2 Feb., 6 Feb., 10 Feb., 14 Feb., 18 Feb., 22 Feb., 26 Feb.
Lucky Days: 7 Feb., 19 Feb.
Misfortune Days: 12 Feb., 24 Feb.
Bad Days: 1 Feb., 3 Feb., 13 Feb., 15 Feb., 25 Feb., 27 Feb

Month 2 in the Dragon Year (6 Mar 24 - 5 Apr 24)

The fate requirements for persons born in the Year of the Rat this month are thought to have virtually reached their lowest point and are still unable to move beyond the shadow of tragedy. As a result, you cannot be reckless and impatient in your professional tasks in order to avoid severe problems. On this occasion, you should perform the following: Before acting, do a thorough analysis and examination of the circumstance. You should also make use of unproductive time by getting out to meet and greet consumers on a regular basis. Talk to and share ideas with those you must deal with. To maintain goodwill so that we may rely on one another in the future. You must be cautious of the latter while signing any official contracts this month, and you should double your diligence to avoid losses.

In terms of job, including business, it is still necessary to support yourself and take care of your own duties to the best of your ability. Do not obstruct the work of others. There is a leak on the salary fortune side. Both income and costs are still minimal. Spending must be limited. Look for methods to generate more income through other channels in order to retain liquidity and keep money in the system.

The family horoscope is pretty accurate. Even if there was some internal conflict, he was able to control it and solve it. Be wary of third parties who will cause divides in your love life at this period. As a result, you should be wary of the appearance of a major debate.

Your health is deteriorating. Be cautious of the rapidly changing weather. It will result in colds or allergies. Furthermore, your health will be tedious and feeble this month. As a result, sickness may readily interfere and make individuals sick. During this time, be wary of new pals who may try to dupe you into spending your money.

There will be consequences for beginning a new career, investing in stocks, and making other risky investments.

Support Days: 1 Mar., 5 Mar., 9 Mar., 13 Mar., 17 Mar., 21 Mar., 25 Mar., 29 Mar.
Lucky Days: 2 Mar., 14 Mar., 26 Mar.
Misfortune Days: 7 Mar., 19 Mar., 31 Mar.
Bad Days: 8 Mar., 10 Mar., 20 Mar., 22 Mar

Month 3 in the Dragon Year (6 Apr 24 - 5 May 24) This month, the Lord Destiny's life path advances in the direction of recharging. The surface of the horoscope is like the sky after a rainstorm, exposing a brilliant rainbow. brave to think, brave to act on what you believe and intend to do this month. When you have made your decision, you should proceed and do your best. You don't have to listen to the protesters. As a result, you won't pass up any fantastic possibilities that come your way.

In terms of employment, especially business, this is a moment of profitable opportunity, so as the tide rises, hurry and work tirelessly to produce results and generate sales. You will meet the conditions for promotion and a better wage if you combine your knowledge and talent with diligence and drive. This includes establishing a new career, buying stocks, and making other investments. Adding more branches is achievable since you will have strong sponsors or partners to invest in. This includes obtaining good and satisfying returns.

As for the fortune of this wage, even though the income is gradual and not outstanding, if you dare to embrace the possibilities that come your way and go ahead to achieve your objective, you will be rewarded. Money will be waiting for you ahead.

The family horoscope for this month is calm. Everyone, including family and friends, will find people to support and assist them. The connection is easy in terms of love. There will be possibilities to travel or join in volunteer activities to aid others during this period, which will help to establish relationships in another way.

In terms of health, the body is robust and in good condition. Just be cautious of mishaps caused by equipment or machinery. It might result in hand or limb injuries.

Support Days: 2 Apr., 6 Apr., 10 Apr., 14 Apr., 18 Apr., 22 Apr., 26 Apr., 30 Apr.
Lucky Days: 7 Apr., 19 Apr.
Misfortune Days: 12 Apr., 24 Apr.
Bad Days: 1 Apr., 3 Apr., 13 Apr., 15 Apr., 25 Apr., 27 Apr

Month 4 in the Dragon Year (6 May 24 - 5 Jun 24)
This month's horoscope for people born in the Year of the Rat is also on the rise. During this time, obstacles and difficulties that have caused accumulated discomfort will be rectified and resolved. As a result, throughout this time, you should analyze your own preparation in all aspects. Fill it up as soon as possible. If a favorable chance presents itself, you will be ready to battle again. If you dare to act, the outcomes will be lucrative and you will be able to attain your objectives. The labor and willpower that goes into it will not be wasted.

This wage fortune is pouring more thickly than it was previously. Since last month, funds have been flowing in two directions regularly. You will receive more riches if you enhance your vigilance. It is also an excellent time for new and old investments, such as purchasing a franchise, combining a corporation, or purchasing stock. You will be rewarded how you desire.

Work, especially commercial industry, has discovered a way to success. If every component joins forces to move the project ahead. The job will be even better than before. If you're still undecided, this is a fantastic chance. If you ignore it, you may come to regret it till the end of the year. There is a potential that those of you working this month may hear positive news at work. Have the possibility to expect for a raise in pay or a promotion to a higher-level post.

The horoscope for the family is serene, and favorable power has arrived. This month's home offers the opportunity to greet significant guests as well as new members. Both are excellent dates to get engaged, married, or propose to your loved one. You will not be disappointed if you select a time this month.

In terms of health, despite being in good shape, be wary of the reappearance of congenital illnesses. Keep an eye out for gastritis. Infectious intestinal disorders, skin problems, and unanticipated accidents are all possibilities.

Support Days: 4 May., 8 May., 12 May., 16 May., 20 May., 24 May., 28 May.
Lucky Days: 1 May., 13 May., and 25 May.
Misfortune Days: 6 May., 18 May., 30 May
Bad Days: 7 May., 9 May., 19 May., 21 May., 31 May.

Month 5 in the Dragon Year (6 Jun 24 - 6 Jul 24)
This month, the route of your life, born in the Year of the Rat, travels to the line of retribution. As a result, the fateful direction turns and falls down. Something that was going well for the

last month has now deteriorated to the point where you feel heavy and fatigued. Every step on the journey to work must be error-free. Don't allow your boat sink when it's moored or when the work is finished but it doesn't operate correctly, since this may cause significant harm.

You should do the following on this occasion: Bring back part of your investments to maintain liquidity. You should support and accomplish your responsibilities properly. You should also use caution when speaking. Avoid speaking things that are disrespectful or taking advantage of people. It will drive irritable individuals to create issues, obstruct, and bully you, causing you to suffer. A job contract should be thoroughly reviewed for correctness and information before signing. Otherwise, you may come across a con artist who will defraud you of your money.

This pay fortune is a loss of riches. Do not lend money to anyone or sign any form of financial promise. Gambling is one of them. Do not knowingly engage in unlawful business or copyright infringement.

Family horoscopes are concerned with the safety and wellbeing of the family members. Be wary about losing valuables to robbers. There will be disagreements on the side of love. There will undoubtedly be a schism if each party feels they are correct and refuses to give in to the other.

Your horoscope is powerful and healthy. However, be wary with elevated blood pressure. Infectious illnesses caused by consuming fatty foods

In terms of beginning a new employment, It is not a good idea to invest in stocks and other types of investments. If you can prevent it, do so that it is not harmed.

Support Days: 1 Jun., 5 Jun., 9 Jun., 13 Jun., 17 Jun., 21 Jun., 25 Jun., 29 Jun.
Lucky Days: 6 Jun., 18 Jun., 30 Jun
Misfortune Days: 11 Jun., 23 Jun.

Bad Days: 2 Jun., 12 Jun., 14 Jun., 24 Jun., 26 Jun.

Month 6 in the Dragon Year (7 Jul 24 - 7 Aug 24)

Your destiny, born in the Year of the Rat, appears to be unsettled as you enter this month. When a month doesn't support us, the journey isn't as smooth as it used to be. Business activities are frequently hampered by impediments and challenges. Even when there is a good opportunity, decision making is typically slower than others. As a result, the task is frequently taken first by expert hands.

You should make yourself a trustworthy person this month by keeping your word and saying everything you say. Don't turn around. Otherwise, those who wish to contact you will be distrustful. Being skeptical of him to the extent of passing up a wonderful work chance.

In terms of work, you will face blocking and obstacle from people who do not intend to do so during this time. There will be disagreements and confrontations with coworkers. As a result, you should maintain your cool in your fortress. You should keep your emotions under control and be as alert as possible. Don't make oneself too noticeable. People will not be irritated. Putting oneself through unnecessary pain and harm.

Financial fortunes are very constant, with direct income pouring in usually. But you must not be greedy if you want to make money through gambling, gambling, or fortune telling. Because there is a greater risk of injury. You should also look for strategies to increase your revenue. However, if you expect to make a fortune in criminal business this month, you may end up in prison.

There is a lack of harmony in the household. Because there will be an occurrence that will have an impact on the individuals in the house.

There is nothing to be concerned about when it comes to lovely love. However, when it comes to health, you must be cautious since concealed diseases will arise and assault. In addition to paying greater attention to your health, you must also be cautious about workplace and road-related injuries.

In terms of beginning a new career, investing in stocks, and making other decisions. This month is not going well.

Support Days: 3 Jul., 7 Jul., 11 Jul., 15 Jul., 19 Jul., 23 Jul., 27 Jul., 31 Jul.
Lucky Days: 12 Jul., 24 Jul.
Misfortune Days: 5 Jul., 17 Jul., 29 Jul.
Bad Days: 6 Jul., 8 Jul., 18 Jul., 20 Jul., 30 Jul.

Month 7 in the Dragon Year (8 Aug 24 - 7 Sep 24)
This month, the factors for your fate have arrived at the alliance line. It is also empowered by fortunate stars that circle and shine on the house of destiny. As a result, some of the stressful conditions are alleviated. It is safe to say that the monsoon season has ended. As a result, many things have returned to normal

and may again go forward. Work will go smoothly. The trade business will develop and flourish. To effectively overcome challenges, you should shake off prior mistakes, think afresh, try new things, and constantly evolve and progress during this month.

In terms of employment, it is a prosperous path since you will gain auspicious power and discover benefactors to assist and advance you. You should move quickly to carry out your strategy in order to meet your objectives. Dare to go on, and you will find a success milestone waiting for you.

For this pay, fortune is abundant. Income will come in a variety of forms. The more industrious you are, the more wealthy you will be. It's as though no matter what sort of seed you plant, you'll get wonderful returns.

The family riches is tranquil and has patronage power to visit. As a consequence, the family will be full with happy grins.

When it comes to love, the sky is the heart. If you want to take the relationship to the next level. You must make more time and visit more frequently.

There is no such thing as good or bad health. However, you should still be cautious about high blood pressure and eye illness. You should obtain adequate sleep to boost your immunity.

Family and friend horoscopes When difficulties develop, you continue to receive excellent assistance. Throughout the month, people are encouraged to volunteer together to benefit society.

There is a favorable trend in terms of beginning a new career, buying stocks, and making other investments.

Support Days: 4 Aug., 8 Aug., 12 Aug., 16 Aug., 20 Aug., 24 Aug., 28 Aug.
Lucky Days: 5 Aug., 17 Aug., 29 Aug
Misfortune Days: 10 Aug., 22 Aug.

Bad Days: 1 Aug., 11 Aug., 13 Aug., 23 Aug., 25 Aug.,

Month 8 in the Dragon Year (8 Sep 24 - 7 Oct 24)
The fate of individuals born in the Year of the Rat this month has not yet escaped the black darkness that blankets the mansion of destiny. It is because the zodiac house has shifted to meet the opposition line, causing the fate graph to plummet downwards. Furthermore, the unlucky stars are focusing on and harassing those in the house of destiny. The Tai Im star, Xiang Ae star, and the nine stars all attacked. As a result, in addition to having to bear the load of properly updating your existing work. There are still chaotic events that interfere and agitate. You should perform the following this month: Should be nice and modest. Don't go about judging people. To escape the threats that will resurface.

In terms of employment, we faced monsoons throughout this time period. There are issues all over the place. They are continuously dealing with personal issues. You will encounter persons who are surreptitiously promoting discord, as well as others who are rebellious and make it difficult for you to control. Furthermore, when signing any contract paperwork, one must be cautious not to put oneself at a disadvantage.

Starting a new career, buying stocks, and making other investments are all options. This month is not the appropriate time. As a result, it should be postponed first.

This salary fate is not favorable. The income is modest. Expenses are out of control. Both should be wary of capital outflow leakage locations. As a result, you should cut back on needless costs. Plan your spending carefully. Do not gamble, speculate, or calculate your riches.

Family horoscope: Be mindful of the health of the elderly in the home, as well as little details. But they battled and debated until it became a major issue.

A third person will emerge in the center of your love horoscope during this era. You must have good mental and physical control. Don't be careless and act erratically.

In terms of health, keep an eye out for seasonal disorders as well as numerous infectious infections. This includes encountering danger and harm when traveling.

Support Days: 1 Sep, 5 Sep., 9 Sep, 13 Sep, 17 Sep., 21 Sep., 25 Sep., 29 Sep.
Lucky Days: 9 Sep., 22 Sep.
Misfortune Days: 3 Sep., 15 Sep., 27 Sep.
Bad Days: 4 Sep., 6 Sep., 16 Sep., 18 Sep., 28 Sep., 30 Sep

Month 9 in the Dragon Year (8 Oct 24 - 6 Nov 24)
This month's horoscope will be both positive and negative. While there are auspicious stars, there are also negative stars that interfere with the zodiac sign, causing disputes and reversals in work and business. What you should do on this occasion is not meddle with other people's

tasks and avoid dredging up anyone's previous difficulties. Maintain humility in your interactions with both superiors and subordinates. This includes contacting the persons you need to contact. Maintain your authenticity and honesty. Furthermore, please keep in mind that doing good without standing out might be dangerous.

In terms of love, you must be cautious with your words this month. Don't be so charming or personal with the opposite sex that folks at home misinterpret it and cause a split. Furthermore, conflicts may arise during this time, resulting in arguments. As a result, you should avoid using extensions to extend your hair.

 The financial outlook for this month is mild. However, in the commercial world, one must use caution while communicating disparities. It will be the source of future problems.

This month is better for planning than investing if you want to join a joint venture.

For a happy family, but in terms of health, avoid food poisoning, back pain, knee pain, and other ailments that will be inquired about. The best method is to schedule some mild exercise time. It will assist you in becoming stronger. Relatives and friends are excellent. However, be careful not to upset people by saying too much.

Support Days: 3 Oct., 7 Oct., 11 Oct., 15 Oct., 19 Oct., 23 Oct., 27 Oct., 31 Oct.
Lucky Days: 4 Oct., 16 Oct., 28 Oct.
Misfortune Days: 9 Oct., 21 Oct.
Bad Days: 10 Oct., 12 Oct., 22 Oct., 24 Oct.

Month 10 in the Dragon Year (7 Nov 24 - 6 Dec 24)
Enter this month because the favorable stars are leaving their orbits and the zodiac houses are approaching the malignant line. As a result, Destiny's might has dwindled. Work doesn't appear to be moving in the same direction this

month, like a creature with a tiger's head and a snake's tail. There is a lack of cohesion. Work and business will be hampered by unanticipated hurdles, and blunders will be common. What you should do this month is to dare to come forward and accept responsibility if anything goes wrong at work during this time period. Otherwise, it will harm your reputation and undermine your trust.

We all face threats and challenges in the world of business and commerce. Both discovered individuals with malicious intent who deceive and swindle. Furthermore, disputes arose in the line of command. As a result, the designated individual should go in and examine himself to reduce errors. You must use extreme caution while signing any paperwork for employment.

This income has been through a hurricane in terms of fortune, earning a little and paying a lot. Keep an eye out for unusual money outflows. Reduce needless costs and look for methods to boost your income to easily balance your budget. There will be no shortage of funds.

You should also avoid gambling. Don't be greedy if you don't want to fall victim to fraudsters.

The family's horoscope is not peaceful. You should monitor the elderly's health and be cautious of mishaps that may occur in the house.

Arguments about terrible love are common. You must be cautious of third parties who may cause havoc and avoid becoming infected with love-related disorders.

Be cautious of liver illness, heart disease, and high blood pressure. Accidents when traveling, family and friends, beginning a new career, investing in stocks and other financial instruments. This month is not going well. You should avoid it.

Support Days: 4 Nov., 8 Nov., 12 Nov., 16 Nov., 20 Nov., 24 Nov., 28 Nov.
Lucky Days: 9 Nov., 21 Nov.
Misfortune Days: 2 Nov., 14 Nov., 26 Nov.

Bad Days: 3 Nov., 5 Nov., 15 Nov., 17 Nov., 27 Nov., 29 Nov.

Month 11 in the Dragon Year (7 Dec 24 - 5 Jan 25)

This month's destiny criterion for people born in the Year of the Rat is that the skies will open in your favor. As a result, it is regarded as a favorable indicator that many of the accumulated stuck difficulties will begin to alter in a positive manner. The finish is smooth and brilliant. As a consequence, work, especially commercial companies, will have an easier time getting through. Businesses will discover new revenue-generating options with a promising future. Those who work on a regular basis during this time will be encouraged and supported by adults. As a result, if you completed a project during this time, now is a terrific moment to present it. It will seem as a merit that has the potential to increase your position. However, there are several things you should do on this occasion: Study prior failures as lessons, repair them, then take new actions and enhance your boldness in presenting work or picking new investment channels that will yield high results.

In terms of fortune, this wage has increased. Income is plenty, but one should not be overly greedy with excessive expectations. Including outlawing gambling, gambling, or wanting to earn rich quickly by undertaking unlawful enterprise. Because there will be more negative consequences.

The family horoscope for this month is calm. However, the love tale encountered a stumbling block. A third party will intervene to generate complications and confusion.

In terms of health, he is in terrific shape throughout this time. The shifting weather conditions will cause relatively mild ailments.

In terms of beginning a new career, investing in stocks, and making other decisions. Simply pick the best one. Invest in good times and you can certainly expect dividends.

Support Days: 2 Dec., 6 Dec., 10 Dec., 14 Dec., 18 Dec., 22 Dec., 26 Dec., 30 Dec.
Lucky Days: 3 Dec., 15 Dec., 27 Dec
Misfortune Days: 8 Dec., 20 Dec.
Bad Days: 9 Dec., 11 Dec., 21 Dec., 23 Dec.

Amulet for The Year of the Rat
"The God Cheng Dao Zhou"

This year, those born in the Year of the Rat should set up and revere religious things. Place "God Heng Jia sits on a throne" on your work desk or cash register to beg for His might and prestige to assist guard the person of your destiny from any hazards that will arise from the unfortunate stars that will befall you. This year's events will fade into obscurity. Blessed with excellent fortune Throughout the year, you will be blessed with excellent fortune and money.

(Note: The inscription at the conclusion of your life cycle shows the direction in which religious artifacts should be placed.)

A chapter in the Department of Advanced Feng Shui discusses the gods who will come to reside in the mia keng (house of fate) for the year. They are gods that can bring both good and misfortune to the lord of fate that year. When this is the case, worship will improve your luck with the gods that visit you on your birthday.

As a consequence, it is said to have the best outcomes and have the greatest impact on you in order to rely on the might of that deity to assist safeguard and protect you. There are calamities to relieve while your fortunes deteriorate. At the same time, I'd want to pray for blessings for you to help your business run smoothly and bring you and your family wealth.

Those born in the year of the Rat or Mia Keng (house of fate) belong to the zodiac sign Tzu. This year, you must be able to assess individuals. Don't judge someone just on their appearance. Be wary about getting duped. Work and finances need careful consideration at all times. Consider all considerations before proceeding, and don't forget to consider the health of the adults in the house. In terms of fortune, there will be reasons of wealth loss owing to unanticipated circumstances.

"God Qi Tian Da Shen" as well as "God Heng Jia sits on a throne." This is considered the final chapter in which he is endowed with strong abilities. Those born in the Year of the Rat this year will endure many challenges, according to their horoscope. It will be critical to understand how to adjust to the scenario, location, and time. Because events frequently have novel structures. Come in so that you may address the situation. God Heng Jia, who has the ability to morph into seventy-two different forms and the ability to shake the sky, frequently assists the monkeys. If the Year of the Rat is summoned, place "God Heng Jia sits on a throne" at home or at work. It will assist to fill up the gaps, giving you the power and bravery to face challenges and issues, as well as acute intellect. It also encourages your work duties and business to run smoothly, to grow, and to have satisfactory sales. Have excellent health and vigor, and be free of calamity and sadness.

Those born in the Year of the Rat should also wear an auspicious pendant. Wear "God Heng Jia sits on a throne" around your neck or carry it with you when traveling both near and far from home. Prosperity and growth in commerce and trade are required for the owner of his destiny to be filled with money and auspicious places. All year, the family is tranquil and joyful. It generates greater and faster efficiency and effectiveness than previously.

Good Direction: Southeast, North, and Southwest
Bad Direction: South
Lucky Colors: Blue, Gray, Blue, White, Gold, and Silver
Lucky Times: 07.00 – 08.59, 15.00 – 16.59, 23.00 – 02.59.
Bad Times: 11.00 – 11.59, 13.00 – 14.59, 17.00 – 18.59.

Good Luck For 2024

Made in the USA
Las Vegas, NV
07 January 2024

83996420R10042